Introduction

The area covered by the this guide is bisected by the A9 – the road that runs all the way from Stirling to Thurso in Caithness. To the east of the road is the green and rolling farmland on the Black Isle and the hammer-head peninsula of Easter Ross. To the west, the lowlands quickly give way to the highland wilderness of Easter Ross. There are few roads and few settlements in the hills. You could walk from Alness to Ullapool on the west coast without crossing a public road.

The guide's western boundary, therefore, is not well defined – it roughly follows a line up the centre of the country. The northern boundary is clearer: the long southern shore of the Dornoch Firth. The southern boundary is the north shore of the Moray Firth and Beauly Firth. The third of the great sea inlets in this area is the Cromarty Firth, which separates the Black Isle from Easter Ross.

The main service centre for the area is Inverness, just to the south. The largest towns are Dingwall, Alness, Invergordon and Tain.

The Black Isle, as all commentators note, is neither black nor an island, but a peninsula with a low, narrow neck. Travellers in the past could be forgiven for treating it as an island. Journeying north, they would have arrived by boat, across the Kessock Ferry, and left across the Nigg Ferry. The former is no more, replaced by the Kessock Bridge in 1982. The Nigg Ferry still operates in the summer.

There have been several explanations for the 'black' part of the name. The simplest is mistranslation. In Gaelic, 'Eilean Dubhtaich' (*the island of Duthac* – a notable local saint) sounds very similar to 'Eilean Dubh' (*the black isle*).

The bulk of the low ground east of the A9 lies on a base of Old Red Sandstone. On the eastern sides of the peninsulas this forms a line of low cliffs, broken in places to allow small fishing villages such as Rockfield *(Walks 4,5)* and Balintore *(5,6)* and the narrow entrance to the Cromarty Firth. These cliffs end at the twin villages of Rosemarkie *(25,26)* and Fortrose *(23)*, and the strange, narrow headland of Chanonry Point *(24)*. Sandstone is a sedimentary rock, and much of it is fossil-bearing. Cromarty, the handsome village at the tip of the Black Isle, was the home of Hugh Miller, the famous 19th-century geologist. His interest was sparked by the fossils he found at local sites such as South Sutor *(27)* and Eathie *(29)*.

Behind the cliffs the shores of the firths are low, and marked by sand dunes and mud flats *(11,18)*. The high ground to the west is of igneous and volcanic rocks, reaching its highest point at the summit of Ben Wyvis *(13)* – a magnificent viewpoint for the whole area.

The first settlements in the area have been dated to around 6000BC; the first wave of Celts arrived in about 2500BC. Over the following centuries there was more Celtic immigration. Iron Age forts, like the one on Ord Hill above North Kessock *(20)*, are a feature of the area, and suggest that they were a warlike people. The Roman arrival in Britain gives us the first written description of these tribes. They called them the 'Pictii' (*painted/tattooed people*), or Picts. Easter Ross was a Pictish heartland, and their intricately carved stones, from pre-Christian and Christian times, can be found throughout the area *(5)*.

The Romans never established a base in the north, and are said to have lost an entire legion in a disastrous military adventure. There is evidence of a Roman marching camp just north of Portmahomack *(3)*. Could this have been where the lost legion met its end?

The Picts and Scots were united in 843AD. The new kingdom faced an immediate threat from the Vikings, who eventually occupied most of Northern Scotland. (The name 'Dingwall' is from 'thing-vollr', the Norse term for a meeting place or parliament site.)

There was warfare between the Scots and the Vikings for almost 400 years. Macbeth (not the villain portrayed by Shakespeare but a wise and successful ruler) was probably born in Dingwall, in about 1010AD. He successfully defended his kingdom against both Norse and Saxon incursions, and until his death Easter Ross was a significant political centre. His successor, Malcolm Canmore, shifted the centre of power southwards, and this area, though never exactly a backwater, lost its position at the heart of Scottish politics.

Malcolm did, however, grant a charter to Tain *(7)* in 1066. This was probably in connection with the much-venerated shrine of St Duthac. In the 15th century, James IV made so many pilgrimages to Tain that the Nigg Ferry became known as the King's Ferry.

Easter Ross shared in the troubles of the Highlands – clan warfare, the Jacobite risings, the Clearances. Carbisdale *(1)* saw a decisive battle in the Civil War and the glens contain their share of deserted settlements *(8)*. In spite of these upheavals, the area has generally been prosperous. There is good agricultural land and there was once a rich fishing industry and trade with the Baltic. Since the 1970s, when these industries were in decline, the Cromarty Firth has become a safe haven for the rigs of the North Sea oil industry and a hub for wind turbine production.

There are hill walks in this guide *(2,9,10,13,20)*, but this is essentially an area of seascapes, wide skies and broad lowland panoramas. If you are lucky, you may see dolphins, deer and an amazing variety of bird life. And whilst no-one can promise sunshine, this is one of the driest places in Britain!

*Hugh Miller's Cottage, Cromarty
(see Walk 27)*

1 Carbisdale Battlefield

A fine forest walk leading to a tranquil lochan then returning past a viewpoint by the site of the Battle of Carbisdale. Good paths and tracks.
Length: **2¼ miles/3.6km**; *Height Climbed:* **165ft/50m**.

O.S. Sheet 21

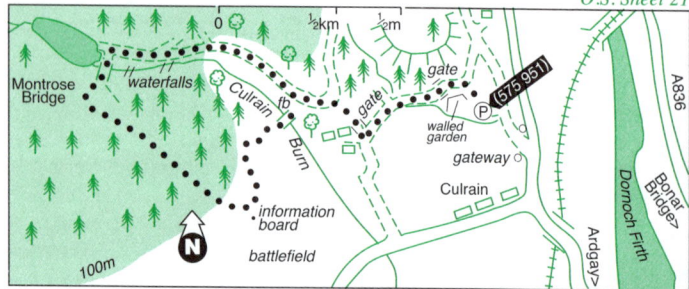

The Marquis of Montrose was one of the great generals of the Civil War, but in 1650 his Royalist army was defeated at the Battle of Carbisdale.

To reach the walk from Tain, take the A836 Bonar Bridge road from the roundabout just south of the Dornoch Firth Bridge. In the centre of Ardgay, look for a minor road signposted for Inveroykel and Carbisdale Forest Walk. Follow the road for 4 miles. There are 3 junctions – go right at each (Inveroykel).

Just beyond the final junction, turn left through a large stone gateway (note a small 'path' sign to the right of the road at this point). Follow a tarred drive for 250m to reach a grassy car park on the left (no sign).

Look for a clear path leaving the car park between large boulders. Follow this to a T-junction and go left on a clear track. You reach a pedestrian gate. Go through this and follow the pleasant track beyond to reach the entrance road to a group of houses. Go right here, climbing to reach a pedestrian gate. Go through this and follow the clear path beyond.

When you reach a junction, keep left. At the next junction, keep straight on, taking note of a wooden footbridge down to your left. This is your return route.

Follow the path as it climbs through woodland, parallel to the burn. Go left at the next junction and continue, passing a series of waterfalls, to reach a secluded lochan.

Cross the embankment at the end of the lochan, then Montrose Bridge. Beyond the bridge, veer right and continue on a rough path through woodland to reach a viewpoint and information board by the battlefield.

From the viewpoint, turn left and follow a clear path through the trees to reach the footbridge. Climb to meet your outward path, turn right and retrace your steps to the start.

2 The Struie_____ B

Struie Hill (known locally as 'the Struie') is a 1200ft/370m hill giving fine views over the Dornoch Firth. This is only a short climb, but it is still a steep hill and rocky in places. Length: **4 miles/6.5km** (there and back); *Height Climbed:* **500ft/150m.**

O.S. Sheet 21

Turn off the A9 just south of Alness at the Struie junction and follow the B9176 for about 12 miles. The road goes over the hill and down into Strath Rory before climbing up to the Struie. This section of road may be closed in the winter – there are snow gates at the start of the high section.

Your objective is obvious as you approach: a long ridge with a craggy face above the road. About half a mile past a large blue sign for a viewpoint there is room to park to the left, below a stand of Scots pines on the Struie (don't block the gateways).

If you are approaching from Tain, take the A836 Bonar Bridge road from the roundabout just south of the Dornoch Firth Bridge. Turn on to the B9176 after about 10 miles. Drive up the hill past the viewpoint and the place to park is about half a mile further on, on the right.

From the parking place, walk north for about 100m (take care, busy road). Just before a road sign look for a rough path cutting off to the right. This leads to an obvious path up the hill and along the edge of the stand of Scots pine. The going is straightforward and you quickly find yourself at the summit cairn. This is the south-western top of the ridge, and the higher of the two, but the best views are from the north-east top.

Walk easily along the ridge. The large boulder is a glacial erratic, dumped here in the last ice age. From the low point of the ridge, follow the track that leads up to the radio mast. There is a fine view down onto the Dornoch Firth – east to the bridge and to Dornoch and west to the Kyle of Sutherland. Return the same way.

3 Portmahomack to Tarbat Ness /
4 Tarbat Ness to Rockfield _____ B/B

3) *An invigorating walk along the Dornoch Firth to the lighthouse at Tarbat Ness, with plenty of opportunities for observing wildlife. Watch out for low-flying aircraft during the week. Length:* **3½ miles/6km** *(one way); Height Climbed:* **50ft/15m**. **4)** *A splendid coastal walk by the Moray Firth, with the chance to see otters, dolphins and a variety of bird life. Length:* **3½ miles/6km** *(one way); Height Climbed:* **100ft/30m**. *These two routes can be combined to make a route of 8 miles/13km (Grade A). Walk 4 can also be linked with Walk 5.*

O.S. Sheet 21

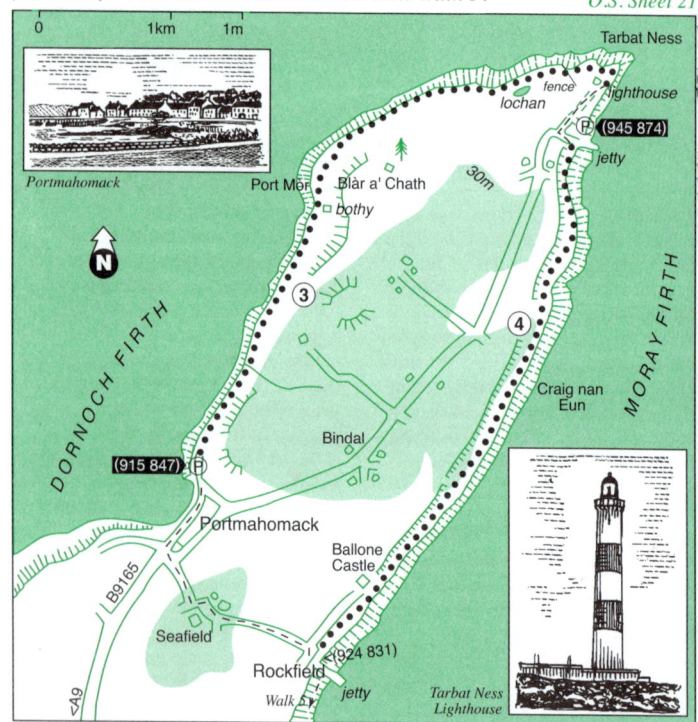

Walk 3) To reach the start of the walk, turn off the A9 about 2 miles south of Tain onto the B9165. Follow this for 9 miles to reach Portmahomack. Keep left when you reach the village, passing a church and continuing along the shore road until it ends at a car park.

From the car park, walk past the houses and through a small gate beside a farm gate. Follow a grass track along the shore. The way is obvious and all but the last of the fences are crossed by stiles or gates.

After about 2 miles/3km the path passes a bothy at Port Mòr and climbs to continue above the rocks. When the cliffs end, return to the shore and pass between a small lochan and the sea. The next fence is the last fence. There is no stile, but **if the tide is low** you can walk round the end of the fence. Continue along the shore and scramble around the rocks at the end of the lighthouse wall to gain a grassy track. This leads round the point and then south to the car park at the start of Walk 4.

If the tide is high, follow the fence inland for about 100m and go through two gates. If you have to make this diversion, you will not be able to get round the end of the wall at the lighthouse. Your best option is to continue following the fence inland, past a small plantation, to a gate. Turn right through the gate and follow the lighthouse wall through a second gate and onto the public road. Turn left to reach the car park at the start of Walk 4.

Walk 4) To reach Tarbat Ness follow the driving instructions for Walk 3 to Portmahomack. Beyond the village, follow the minor road north for about 3 miles to the car park just south of the lighthouse.

Before you start the walk, it is worth taking a trip out to the point. Follow the road to the lighthouse (now on privately-owned ground). A grass track leads beyond to the point. Military aircraft from RAF Tain fly low over the Dornoch Firth and the Tarbat peninsula during the week.

Walk back past the car park to a T-junction and turn left down to a jetty. On the right, a wooden gate opens onto a path that runs easily across the turf and below low red cliffs. The route is generally straightforward walking along the shore, but after about ³/₄ mile/1km the way becomes difficult, and impassable if the tide is in. Here a path leads to the top of cliffs, along the cliff top for a short distance, then back down to the shore.

Continue along the shore to Rockfield. Watch out for Craig nan Eun – 'the cliff of the birds', the highest point of the cliffs and a bird nesting site (**NB:** the birds can be aggressive from May to July) – and for the impressive 16th-century Ballone Castle, now a private house.

If you wish to make a circuit with Walk 3, follow the public road from Rockfield for about 1 mile/1.6km to the T-junction with the B9165. Turn right to a triangular junction with a bus shelter then head downhill and turn right along the shore to the start.

5 Hilton to Rockfield   B

This is an easy walk along the shore between two seaboard villages. There is lots to see and no tide to worry about. Length: **5 miles/9km** (one way); *Height Climbed:* none. *There is a possible link with Walks 4 and 3, making a total distance of* **18 miles/29km**.

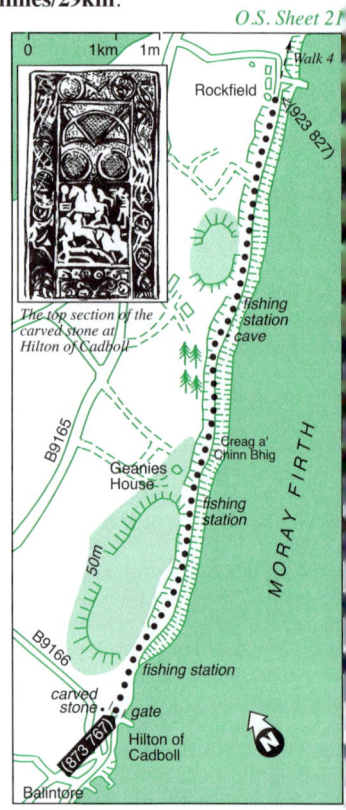

The top section of the carved stone at Hilton of Cadboll

O.S. Sheet 21

Follow directions for the start of Walk 6, but when you come down to the shore, turn left and continue to a car park at the north end of Hilton.

Walk on beyond for a short distance, then turn left and follow the signs for Hilton of Cadboll to a gate by a cattle grid. Beyond this, the Hilton of Cadboll Stone (well worth a visit) is visible to your left. Otherwise, carry straight on, across a field, along the public right of way for Rockfield. The path goes through a kissing-gate then continues through grazing land behind the shore.

Where the cliffs come down, there is a salmon fishing station. The posts by the huts are drying-poles for the nets. A mile/1.6km further on, another salmon station has been converted to a holiday house.

Where the main track curves away uphill, beyond the slanting rocks at Craig a' Chinn Bhig, stick to the track along the shore. Go over a stile and then make a small diversion round a rocky outcrop. The track winds slightly uphill through rocks and then descends. Look back here to see Tarrel Cave. This is an old sea cave, now well above sea level.

You pass another deserted salmon fishing station before the houses of the village of Rockfield come into view ahead. Continue to the gate into the village. Either return by the same route or keep straight on for Walk 4.

6 Balintore & Shandwick _____ C

A short lineal walk connecting two old fishing villages and continuing along a fine sandy beach, with a possible extension to an old well. Length: **3 miles/5km** (there and back); Height Climbed: none.

Turn off the A9 about 2 miles south of Tain and follow the B9165 signposted for Fearn and Portmahomack. At Fearn carry straight ahead onto the B9166. At the T-junction turn left and then almost immediately right, down the hill to Balintore. Turn right at the bottom of the hill and look for the car park just by the harbour. There are information panels in the car park telling you about the villages.

From the car park, follow the shore path south. This leads, in a short distance, to a further car park with more information panels. From here the path onwards is marked as the 'Shandwick Beach Path'. This continues above the beach to the car park in Shandwick.

From here, take the grass track running south along the shore. This is easy walking, beside a sand and shingle beach. You are looking out across the Moray Firth, and on a clear day you can make out the Cairngorm Mountains to the south.

Where the going along the shore gets rough, you can take to the beach or find a stile which takes you over the fence and along a good grass track parallel to the shore. Both ways take you to a seat at the end of the beach.

You can return from this point. If you wish a short extension to visit an old well once thought to have healing

qualities – the Well of Health – then continue along a rough path which climbs across the steep slope above the sea. There's a dilapidated fence of steel poles, driftwood and assorted flotsam and jetsam. The well is in a dip to the right of the path.

7 Two Forest Walks

1) *A short circuit to the summit of Tain Hill, with superb views. Length:* **1⅓ miles/2km**; *Height Climbed:* **260ft/80m**. **2)** *A choice of circuits around a wooded glen with some fine old pine woods. Length: up to* **2 miles/3km**; *Height Climbed:* negligible.

O.S. Sheet 21

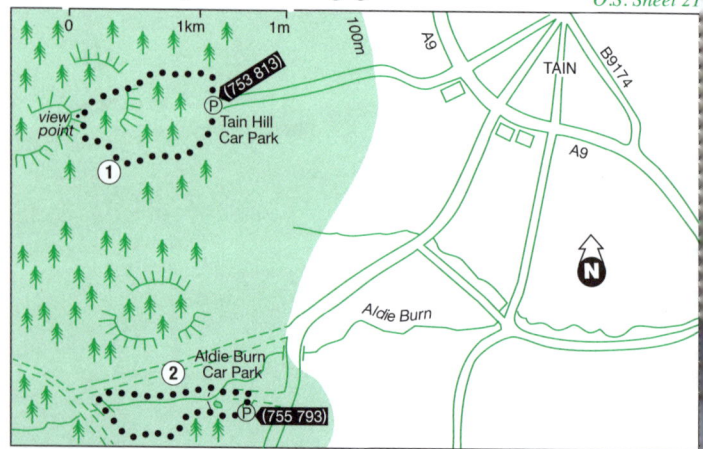

Walk 1) Tain Hill Forest Walk is sign-posted to the west off the A9 just under a mile south of the northern entrance to the town. Turn on to the minor road and follow it for 1 mile to reach the Forestry Commission car park at the end of the road. An information panel shows the route, which is waymarked (red markers) and is all on well-made paths.

Walk north out of the car park and follow the circuit through open, mixed woodland. When you reach Pulpit Rock – the highest point on the walk – you are rewarded with fantastic views over the Dornoch and Cromarty Firths.

Walk 2) The Aldie Burn Forest Walks are signposted to the west off the A9, 1 mile north of the southern entrance to the town. Turn on to the minor road and follow it for 2 miles to reach the Forestry Commission car park to the right of the road.

An information panel in the car park shows two possible waymarked circuits. The **red route** – ½ mile/1km – follows a circuit round a small pond; the **blue route** – 2 miles/3km – makes a longer circuit round the valley of the Aldie Burn through mixed age Scots pine woodland, with some fine old trees along the route.

Both routes follow well-made paths.

8 Strathrory to Scotsburn — B

A lineal walk along the route of an old drove road on tracks and vague paths. Wet and muddy in places. **Length: 4¼ miles/7.4km** *(one way);* **Height Climbed: 260ft/80m.** *NB: Grazing cattle.*

O.S. Sheet 21

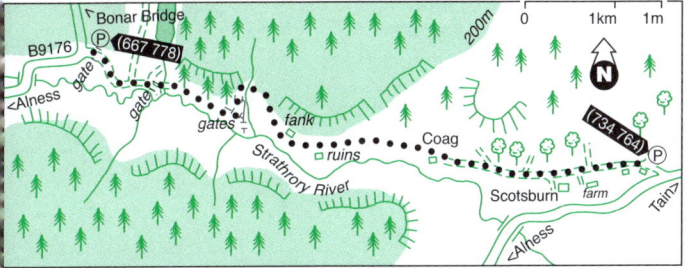

The B9176 for Bonar Bridge leaves the A9 1 mile west of Alness. After 6 miles the road crosses the Strathrory River then climbs. Look for a small sign for the footpath to Scotsburn to the right of the road. There is a car park here.

Walk around a gate and follow the clear track beyond as it drops down and turns left. A track joins from the left. Ignore this and continue. When the track swings hard left, there is a gate straight ahead. Go through this and continue by the river.

The path deteriorates, but your route is not in doubt – continuing with the river to your right and a conifer plantation to your left.

You reach a fence with two gates in it. Go through the left-hand (pedestrian) gate and climb away from the river, with a fence to your right, to reach a further gate. Go through this.

The rough, muddy path continues, now undulating high above the river through scattered trees. There are small burns to cross.

Continue, passing an old sheep fank to your left, then some ruins to your right. When the cottage at Coag comes into view, walk past it to reach a grassy track. Follow this as it becomes clearer and starts to climb, with fine views of the sea opening up.

The track drops, passing through two gates. When it swings right into Scotsburn House, keep straight on through a pedestrian gate. At the next junction, above the farm, keep straight on, passing through a gate to reach a signposted junction just before a further gate.

Ignore the left-hand path (John O'Groats Trail), pass through the gate and continue on the clear path to reach a gate by a row of houses. Go through this and follow the track behind the houses down to a small parking area by the public road and a sign for the footpath to Strath Rory.

9 Cnoc Fyrish

This low hill is distinguished by a curious monument, built in the 18th century to provide work during a period of unemployment. It is also a great viewpoint for the Cromarty Firth and the oil rigs which are usually parked there. Length: **4 miles/6.5km** (there and back); Height Climbed: **900ft/270m**.

O.S. Sheet 21

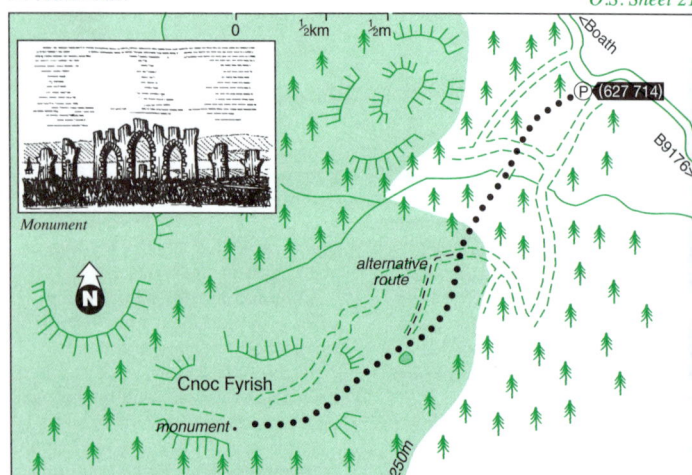

Just west of Alness, turn north off the A9 (or the B817, which runs parallel to it) onto the B9176. After 2 miles turn left on to a minor road, signposted for Boath. There is also a wooden sign for the Fyrish Monument. After about a mile there is a car park on the left with a sign for the Novar Estate – Jubilee Path to the Fyrish Monument.

The path gives a well-marked and pleasant walk through open forest. After crossing a gorge, there is a steepish ascent to a small lochan. Beyond the lochan you are on open hillside and you can look out over the Cromarty Firth.

The monument on the summit is a replica, or at least an imitation, of the gates of the Indian city of Negapatam. The construction was financed by Sir Hector Munro of Novar (Novar House is to the south of the hill), who had captured the city from the Dutch in 1781, following a month-long siege.

Descend the same way. From the lochan, an alternative descent is signposted but this has nothing special to commend it.

10 The Novar Wind Farm —————————————————— A

This walk is a hi-tech spectacular with great views as a bonus. The distance given is to Bendeallt, but you can go further (or not as far) if you wish. Choose a clear day. Length: **7 miles/11km** (there and back); Height Climbed: **1200ft/360m.**

O.S. Sheet 21

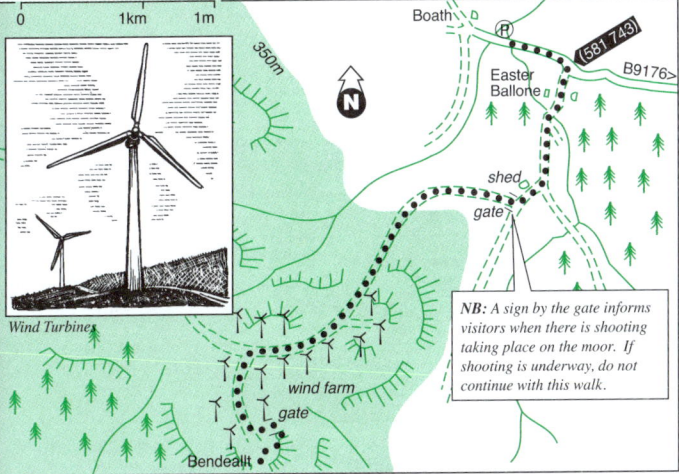

Wind Turbines

NB: *A sign by the gate informs visitors when there is shooting taking place on the moor. If shooting is underway, do not continue with this walk.*

The walk up to the wind farm is straightforward, but avoid extreme weather conditions, especially thunderstorms and icy weather, and don't climb the access ladders up the turbines: a fall could be fatal.

Follow the directions for Walk 9 but continue beyond the car park for a further 3½ miles, where a track heads off left to Ballone. Continue along the road for a short distance to find a parking area to the right of the road then walk back and turn up the track.

Follow the track past the farm buildings. When the track forks keep to the right and climb to the wind farm shed. Just beyond this the track splits. Go right, through a gate, and climb to the turbines.

Walk through the turbines, ignoring tracks to right and left, until the main track passes through a fence. At the next junction, immediately beside turbine 27 (they are all numbered), turn left and follow the track to its end at turbine 19.

Look left from the turbine to find a gate in a fence. Go through this to reach the open moor, then either turn right to reach the visible peak of Bendeallt, or simply enjoy the wonderful views then return the same way.

11 Kiltearn Church & Balconie Point

This walk goes along a quiet road, past a ruined church and graveyard and out to Balconie Point. If you fancy a shorter walk, you can make your way back along the banks of the River Sgitheach. Length: **3 miles/5km**; *Height Climbed:* none.

O.S. Sheet 21

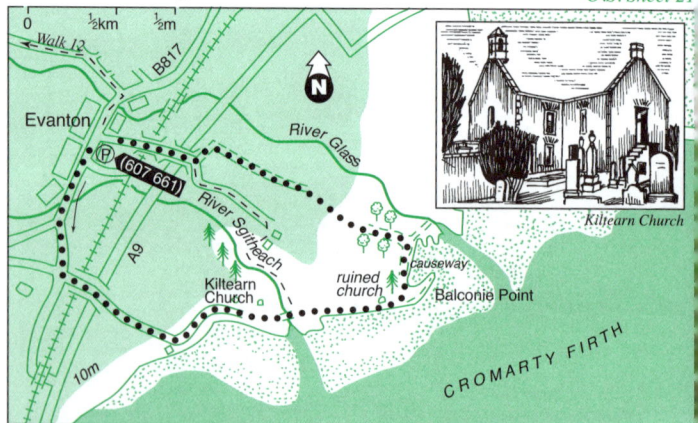

Kiltearn Church

From the car park in the middle of Evanton, walk south along the main street following a sign for the Kiltearn Church Circular Walk. Follow the road out of town and cross over at the war memorial to stay on a pavement. About ¾ mile/1km from the car park, turn left at the crossroads (a bad crossing: take care) and follow a minor road across bridges over the railway and A9 and on to the shore.

The road turns left by the shore and passes the ruined church. The old graveyard is worth exploring before continuing by the shore on a grass path. A footbridge takes you over the River Sgitheach.

At this point a signposted path leads up the river to Evanton, but to continue to Balconie Point, continue around the shore past a second, much smaller, ruined church. At the point, there is a trig point and a small plantation. Walk round the plantation and follow the path away from the shore.

The path follows a causeway between marshy areas. Just beyond these it joins another path. Turn left along this, through trees then across a field. On the far side of the field, continue along the clear grassy track between fields. As it nears the A9 the track swings left, eventually joining a public road. Turn right along the road, crossing the A9 and railway on bridges to return to Evanton.

12 Black Rock Gorge ———————————————— C

*This gorge is 100ft/30m deep and only a few metres wide, with black waters roaring through its depths. The walk is easy, but **great care should be taken by the gorge edge and when crossing the bridges**. Length:* **2½ miles/4km**; *Height Climbed:* **300ft/90m**.

O.S. Sheet 21

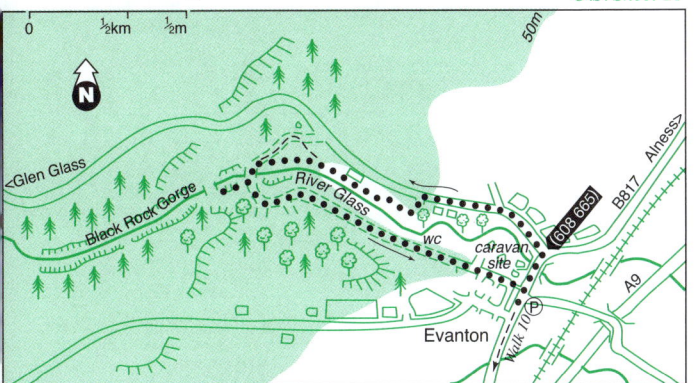

Start from the car park in the centre of Evanton. Walk along the road in the direction of Alness, past the Black Rock Caravan site and over the bridge. Take the road on the left, signposted 'Glenglass'. To the north, you can see the monument on Fyrish Hill (*see* Walk 9).

After about half a mile/0.8km, beyond the last house on the left, look for a path leading down to the river through conifers. At the river, turn right and head upstream. The path follows the river bank then starts to climb as you approach the gorge. At the top of the hill, the path runs close to the edge, so proceed with care.

Where the path forks, the left-hand path (narrow and overgrown) takes you along the edge of the gorge to the first bridge. (If you prefer a gentler alternative, turn right. After about 50m the path joins a broad track. Turn left along the track and after about 150m it ends. Take the path on your left down to the first bridge.)

Cross the bridge and gaze into the murky depths. If you turn right beyond the bridge there is a second bridge, and a second view of the gorge, about 100m upstream.

From the first bridge a path leads downstream, but uphill, to join a second track. Turn left along this to join a forestry track which takes you back to Evanton. When you reach the surfaced road, turn left down a narrow lane to reach the town centre.

Walks Easter Ross & The Black Isle

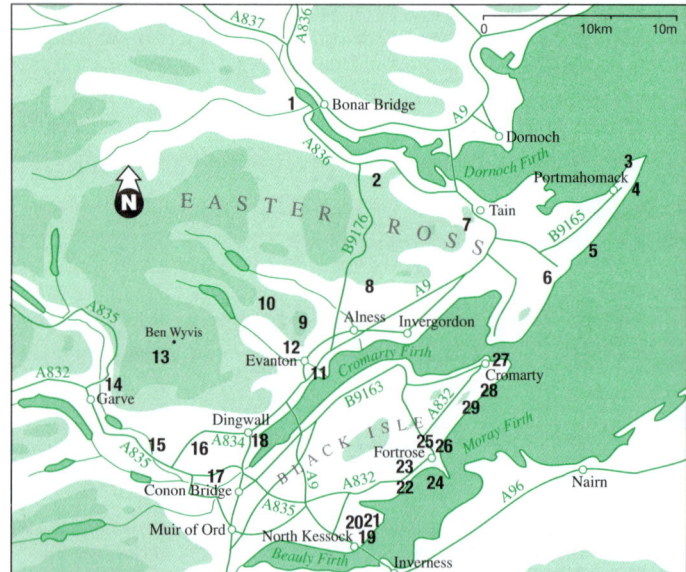

Grades

A+ .. Full walking equipment – including map and compass – and previous hill walking experience essential

A .... Full walking equipment required

B .... Strong walking footwear and waterproof clothing required

C .... Comfortable walking footwear recommended

[**B/C**, etc ...... Split grades refer to the fact that the single route described can be walked either in its entirety or in shorter, less gruelling sections.]

NB: Assume each walk increases at least one grade in winter conditions. Hill routes can become treacherous.

Walks Easter Ross & The Black Isle

walk	grade	walk	grade
1 Carbisdale Battlefield	C	16 Knock Farrel	B/C
2 The Struie	B	17 The Brahan River Walk	B
3 Portmahomack to Tarbat Ness	B	18 Dingwall Shore Path	C
4 Tarbat Ness to Rockfield	B	19 Around Ord Hill	B
5 Hilton to Rockfield	B	20 Ord Hill	B
6 Balintore & Shandwick	C	21 Ord Hill & Kilmuir	B
7 Two Forest Walks	C	22 Ormond Castle & Wood Hill	C
8 Strathrory to Scotsburn	B	23 Fortrose to Avoch	C
9 Cnoc Fyrish	B	24 Chanonry Point	C
10 The Novar Wind Farm	A	25 The Fairy Glen	C
11 Kiltearn Church & Balconie Point	B	26 Scart Craig	B
12 Black Rock Gorge	C	27 South Sutor & The 100 Steps	B
13 Ben Wyvis	A+	28 McFarquhar's Bed	B
14 Silverbridge Forest Trail	C	29 Eathie	B
15 Contin & Rogie Falls	C		

The mouth of the Cromarty Firth from Invergordon

— www.pocketwalks.com

Published by: Hallewell Publications, Scotland
Printed by: Barr Printers Ltd, Glenrothes

While every care has been taken in the preparation of this guide, the publishers cannot accept responsibility for any loss, damage or injury resulting from its use.

13 Ben Wyvis _____ A+

A fine hill climb. Ben Wyvis is perhaps the most spectacular viewpoint on the east coast. The sweeping panorama takes in the mountains of the north-west and the firths of the North Sea coast. Length: **9 miles/14.5km** *(there and back); Height Climbed:* **3000ft/910m**.

O.S. Sheet 20

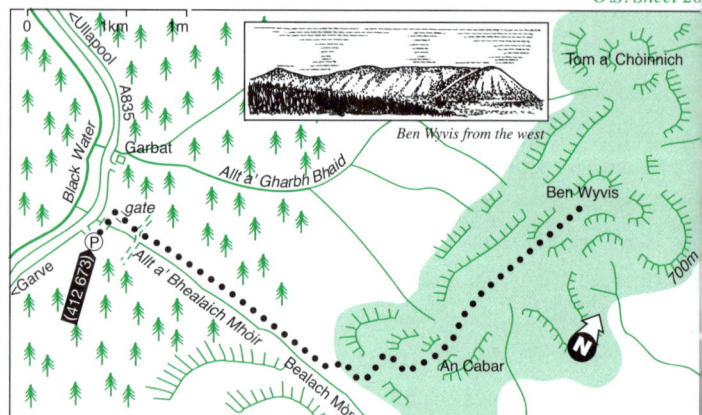

Ben Wyvis from the west

This is a straightforward hill climb on well-maintained paths, but don't underestimate it. Ben Wyvis is a Munro, over 3000ft high, and is subject to sudden changes of weather, so go prepared.

About 4 miles north of Garve on the A835 Ullapool road there is a signposted car park (Ben Wyvis) to the right of the road, just before the bridge over the Allt a' Bhealaich Mhòir.

From the car park, walk north along the clear path parallel to the road. This crosses a footbridge over the river and continues. After a short distance there is a kissing-gate in a deer fence to the right. Go through this and start climbing on a clear path.

The path crosses a forestry road, climbs a flight of steps, then continues through woodland by the stream. As you leave the trees the path levels out and there is a sign for the Ben Wyvis National Nature Reserve.

Enjoy the short respite on the approach to Bealach Mòr, as beyond this the path begins its steep and winding ascent of An Cabar, the spur jutting out below the summit of Ben Wyvis.

When you reach the top of An Cabar the gradient eases and it is a pleasant walk to the summit. Enjoy the views.

Descend the same way.

14 Silverbridge Forest Trail _____ C

A signposted Forestry Commission walk on clear, dry footpaths and tracks, running beside a sequence of river rapids. Length: **2 miles/3km**; Height Climbed: negligible.

O.S. Sheet 20

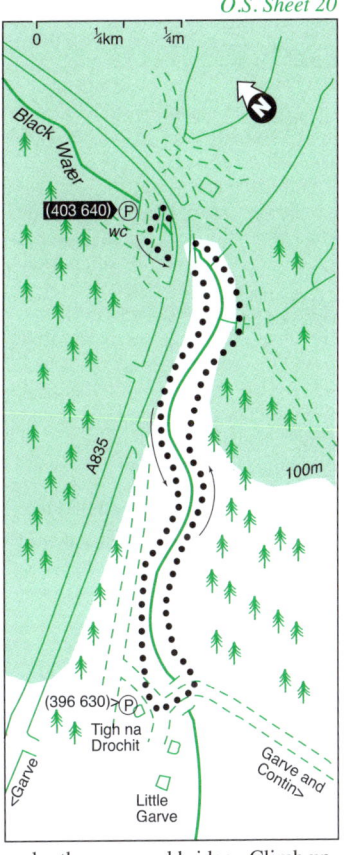

The waters of the Black Water collect in the hilly moorland to the north-west of Ben Wyvis, then flow down the hill's western flank. Just north of Garve, the glen is nipped between the Ben's south-westerly buttress and the low hills to the west, and the river is squeezed into a series of rapids. To reach the start of the walk which follows the river bank at this point, drive north from Garve on the A835. After two miles the road crosses the river. Just before the bridge there is a large car park to the left of the road, by the end of the old road bridge.

Drop down from the car park and follow the signposted path along the river bank, running through a mixed woodland of pine and birch. After a mile/1.6km, the path reaches the furthest extent of the walk, near the smaller car park at Little Garve. Drop down past the cottage at Tigh na Drochit and turn left across the bridge: built in 1762 as part of a network of military roads constructed in the eighteenth century.

At the far end of the bridge there is a signposted junction, with a path indicated to the right leading to Garve. For this route, turn left (signposted for Silverbridge) and follow the path back up the riverside.

The clear path peels away from the river, climbs past a picnic table by a viewpoint, then descends to pass under the new road bridge. Climb up to the old bridge and cross it to return to the start.

15 Contin & Rogie Falls

Two linked groups of signposted Forestry Commission walks on clear tracks. Length: 1/2-2 3/4 miles/0.7-4.5km; Height Climbed: **450ft/140m** (on Contin Green route). *Fine waterfalls at Rogie.*

O.S. Sheet 26

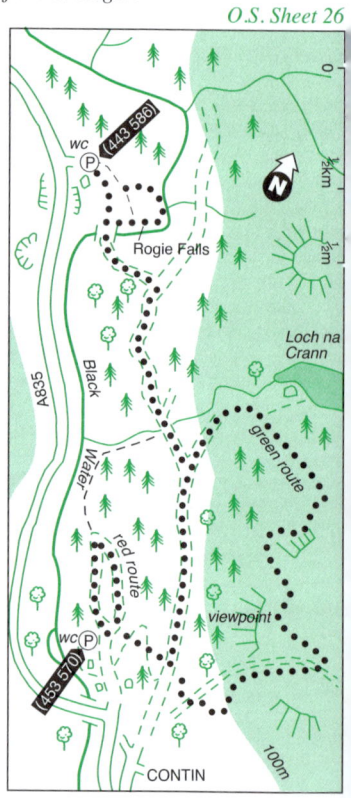

The little village of Contin is 2 miles south-west of Strathpeffer on the A834. To reach the **Contin** walks, drive north from the centre of the village on the A835. Just as the road cuts left, to cross the Black Water, a minor road cuts off to the right, signposted for Contin Forest. Follow this road to the car park, where there is a picnic area and an information board.

There are two signposted routes through the conifer plantations on the slopes above the river. The **Red** route (marked by red-topped posts) is 1/2 mile/0.7km in length; the longer **Green** route is 2 3/4 miles/4.5km in length, and quite steep in places, climbing up to a viewpoint, from where there are fine views of Ben Wyvis (*see* Walk 13) to the north and the pointed peaks of the hills around Strathconon to the west.

In addition, there is a lineal route along a forestry track which links the Contin car park with the routes at Rogie Falls (*see* map). To join this follow the **Green** route until a track splits off signposted for Garve.

To reach **Rogie Falls** by road, drive two miles north from Contin on the A835 and turn right into the signposted car park. The two signposted routes here are both under 1 mile/1.6km in length, and are centred on the dramatic Rogie Falls, which are crossed by a bouncy suspension bridge. Cross this bridge and follow the path beyond to join the footpath to Contin (*see* map).

16 Knock Farrel — B/C

A short climb, steep in places, to the top of a low hill, passing through conifer woodland and farmland. Also, two short forest walks and a possible extension to Dingwall. Length: **1-5 miles/1.5-8km**; *Height Climbed:* **350ft/100m** *(car park to Knock Farrel).*

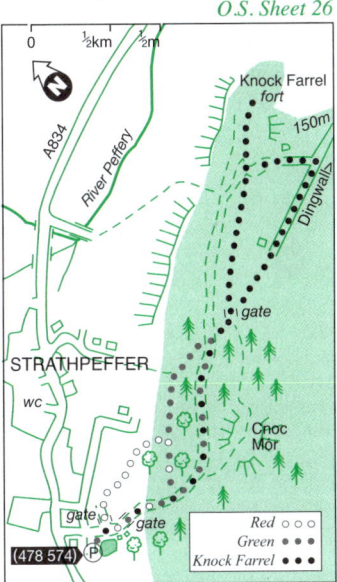

O.S. Sheet 26

To reach the start, drive south from the centre of Strathpeffer (ie, towards Contin and the A832) and watch for a sign pointing left for the Blackmuir Wood Footpaths. Follow the track for a short distance to reach the car park.

There are two signposted paths – a short loop (**red**) and a longer loop (**green**) – plus the path up Knock Farrel. Follow the path from the back-left corner of the car park. When it splits, keep to the left of the pond to join a clear access track. Turn right along this.

The track passes to the left of a group of wooden houses at the end of the pond, goes through a gate, then continues through an area of woodland and bracken. After a short distance a path heads off to the left. For the **red** route, go left (*see map*). For the others, keep on along the main track.

From the furthest point of the **green** route, the hill path heads right from the main track; climbing up to a signposted junction on the high point of the ridge. Go left here and walk along the undulating ridge to the peak of Knock Farrel, topped by the remains of an Iron Age fort.

From the peak, drop back down to the picnic site on the watershed just before the peak and head left on a clear track which leads down to the public road.

A turn to the left at this point will lead you, in 2 miles/3km, to the edge of Dingwall. For this route, however, turn right; following the road to its end, then taking a rough track uphill to the junction on the ridge. Return from here by the original route or by the return routes of the **green** and **red** walks.

17 The Brahan River Walk _____ B

This is a generally easy walk on riverside paths and quiet public roads through Brahan Estate. The distance given is for the full circuit, but you can make your own variations (see map). Length: **9 miles/14.5km**; *Height Climbed:* **230ft/70m**.

O.S. Sheet 26

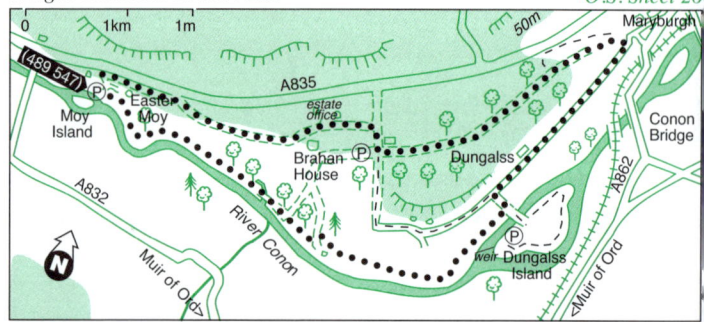

Take the A835 Ullapool road from the roundabout a mile south of Dingwall. After 3¾ miles turn left onto a small road marked Easter Moy. (If you come to the Muir of Ord sign, you've gone too far!) Turn right immediately, at the junction, and follow the metalled road as it swings left down to a parking area by the river.

Go over a stile by a gate and on along a broad track by the river. After a mile/1.6km a small suspension bridge leads onto a broad track. In a short way the track swings hard left. Keep straight on here, on a rough path running parallel to the river.

This quickly joins another track, with a structure visible ahead-right and a signpost. Cross the track (Dunglass Island) and follow a faint path. This soon swings right, with a field fence to your left, before edging left between two fences.

Continue by the field. The river eventually reappears at the foot of a slope to your right, then you continue on the rough path until you join the broad track at the bridge to Dunglass Island. (The path around the island is about 2 miles/3km in length.)

Walk up the track, away from the river, to join a quiet public road. A turn to the left offers a possible shortcut (*see map*), but for this route turn right. After a mile/1.6km you reach the edge of Maryburgh. Watch for a sign for Tallysow Wood and turn left.

After a short distance you reach a junction by an isolated metal gate. Go left here, and follow a fine wooded track (ignoring one path heading off to the right) to a four-way junction with a house to your right.

Go right, then first left (passing the estate office and Brahan House) to return to the start.

18 Dingwall Shore Path   C

A waymarked walk leading from the centre of Dingwall out along the coast of the tidal head of the Cromarty Firth. Plenty of estuarine bird life. **Length: 3 miles/5km**; *Height Climbed:* negligible.

O.S. Sheet 26

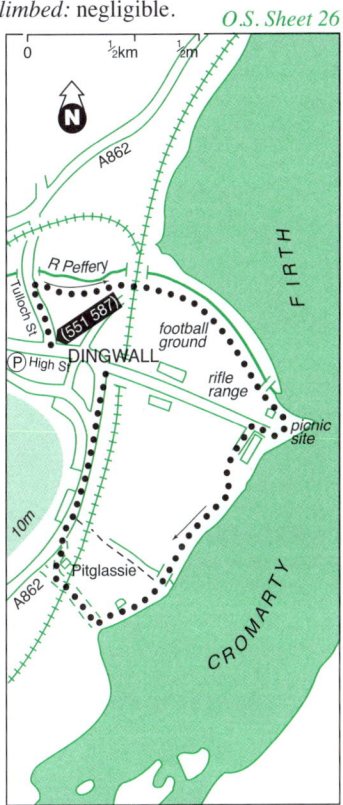

From the east end of the one-way section of Dingwall High St, turn north up Tulloch St and follow it until it crosses the River Peffery, then turn right on the near side of the river, following the clear footpath signposted for Ferry Picnic Site.

When the path reaches a signposted junction go left, across the railway line (take care here) then continue with an area of flat parkland to the right which includes the modern ground of Ross County FC. Near the end of the path there is a military rifle range: if the flag by the path is displayed it will be necessary to turn back at this point.

Continue down to the picnic site at the mouth of the river, from where fine views open up across the Cromarty Firth – muddy at low tide – to the Black Isle.

It is possible to return on either side of the river. To complete the circuit, however, turn away from the shore along a public road, then turn left at a junction, past houses (signposted for the Round Dingwall Walk and Pitglassie). When this ends, continue along a clear footpath.

The path continues, running close by the estuary and giving fine views ahead of the mouth of the River Conon and of the bird life on the mudflats. When the path reaches a hut you have a choice. Either return by the same route or, for a shorter but less scenic return, turn inland up a clear track, recrossing the railway line then continuing to the public road. Turn right to return to the start.

19 Around Ord Hill / 20 Ord Hill / 21 Ord Hill & Kilmuir _____ B/B/B

A series of paths through conifer and broad-leaved woodland, climbing to a wooded summit marked by the remains of an Iron Age fort. These routes can be linked, with the option of returning by the shore of the Moray Firth (Walk 21). **19)** *A circuit of the hill. Length:* **2½ miles/ 4km**; *Height Climbed:* **400ft/120m**. **20)** *A climb to the top of the hill. Length:* **2½ miles/4km** *(there and back); Height Climbed:* **600ft/180m**. **21)** *A path to a shoreside village and back (**NB:** shore path is tidal). Length:* **4 miles/6.5km**; *Height Climbed:* **600ft/180m**.

O.S. Sheet 26

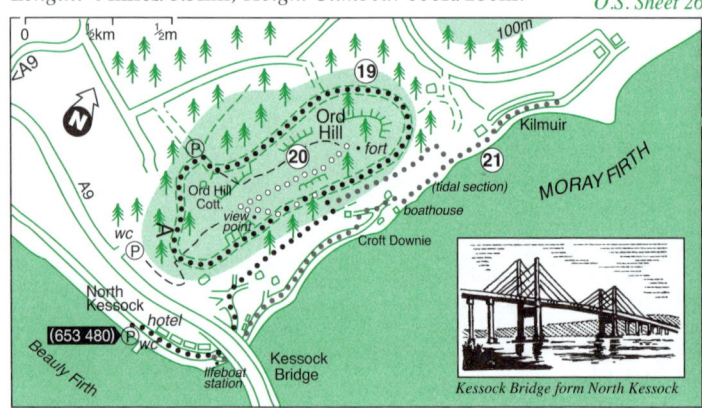

Kessock Bridge form North Kessock

Ord Hill is a low, wooded eminence by the northern end of the Kessock Bridge. The series of paths through the trees can be joined from three points: North Kessock; the car park by the A9, just to the north (accessible from the south-bound carriageway); and the Ord Hill car park (*see* map). In the following descriptions, all routes begin from North Kessock.

North Kessock is the southernmost village in the Black Isle. Nowadays it's often bypassed, although once it was the busy landing point for the Kessock ferry.

From Inverness, drive north up the A9, across the Kessock Bridge, and follow the signs for North Kessock. Park in the car park just before the slipway and walk towards the bridge.

All Walks) Just before the bridge a minor road cuts off to the right. Keep left and follow the road under the bridge and uphill for about ½ mile/0.8km to reach a signpost. Turn right (signposted for Ord Hill). At a hairpin bend go right on a metalled road. When this forks, almost immediately, look for a waymarked path between the two roads.

Follow this path through mixed woodland, teeming with bird life. The path begins to drop quite steeply. After a short distance an unmarked path, faint at first, cuts off to the left, uphill. This climbs, on wooden steps, to a signpost.

Walk 19 & 20) Turn left and climb up to join a forestry road which contours round the hill. This is the 'Ord Hill Circular'.

Walk 19) Turn right and follow the clear, generally level, path which runs around the hill. The route is marked by blue posts and rarely in doubt. For the most part it passes through open conifer woodland, with fine views throughout, particularly of the head of the firth and the hills beyond from the southern end of the hill (*see* below).

There are three signposted paths leading to the fort (*see* map). Otherwise, return by the same route.

Walk 20) When you reach the Ord Hill Circular, turn left. Watch for a track climbing to the right, signposted for the 'View Point'. Turn on to this and follow it past a splendid view point overlooking Inverness and the Kessock Bridge before joining a path up the ridge of the hill. Turn right along this and follow red marker posts to the summit. On the way, you pass through the tumbled remains of Iron Age fortifications.

There is only a limited view from the summit through the trees. Return the same way or follow the red posts down to the north side of the hill.

Walk 21) From the signpost, continue on the path signposted for Kilmuir. This contours at first, then begins to descend gently.

At a sign for the 'Shore Path', turn right and follow steps down the last of the slope. (**NB:** the shore path is tidal in places, and should be avoided at or approaching high tide).

A turn to the left along the shore leads you to the old fishing settlement of Kilmuir. Double back from here and follow the shore back towards North Kessock. Watch for a boathouse on the shore. Turn inland just before this, climbing through trees towards a wooden house. Join a clear track here and turn left. This joins a metalled road at a hairpin bend.

Go right, with a wooden fence to your left. 100 paces beyond the end of the fence go left, on a rough path leading downhill to join a metalled track. Turn right to return to the start.

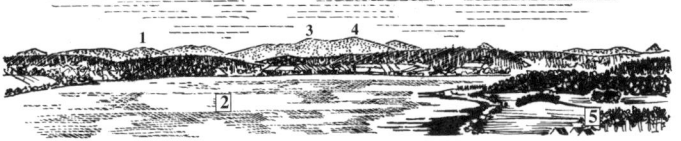

1 *Carn a' Mhuilt (668m)* 2 *Beauly Firth* 3 *Beinn a' Bha'ach Ard (862m)* 4 *Sgurr a' Phollain (855m)*
5 *Charlestown*

22 Ormond Castle & Wood Hill

*An easy circuit through woodland and farmland passing the site of an ancient castle. Fine coastal views. Quiet roads, footpaths and clear tracks. Length: up to **3 miles/5km**; Height Climbed: **210ft/65m**.*

O.S. Sheet 26

Avoch is a former fishing village on the Moray Firth. To reach it, follow the A9 to the roundabout at Tore and take the A832. Follow this for 6 miles. The main road drops down to cross the Avoch Burn. Just before this look for Long Road to the right. Follow this to a junction and go right, now driving along the sea front.

There are parking spaces along the roadside by the shore. Park and continue walking along the road. The road swings right, away from the sea and starts to climb, leaving the village. At the top of the hill, look for a sign for a footpath to Ormond Castle.

Go left, following the drive to Castleton. When the drive swings right, just before a gate into a house, leave it and head half left, passing through the middle of three gates, to reach a grassy path between field fences.

The site of the castle, marked by a flagpole on top of a low hill, is now clearly visible ahead. Follow the path through two gates, then around the base of the hill to reach a pedestrian gate to your right. A plaque here tells the history of the castle. Go through the gate and follow the rough path to the summit from where there are fine views over the Moray Firth.

Return to the gate and go right. You quickly reach a junction on the edge of a conifer wood. Keep straight on (taking note of the path to your right) and follow the clear track as it contours round Wood Hill.

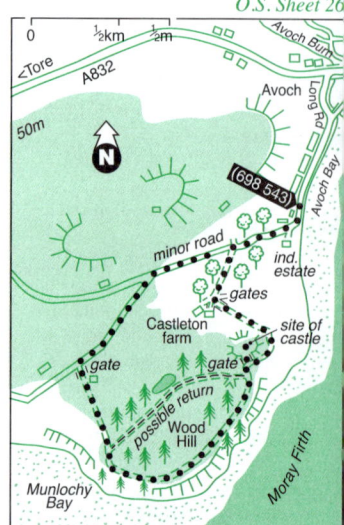

At the end of the wood, a path comes in from the right and a view opens up over Munlochy Bay. It is possible to go right here and follow a clear path back through the wood to the junction and your outward route. Alternatively, carry straight on.

The clear track climbs gently then drops to reach a gate/barrier at its end. Go through the gate and turn right on the tarred road beyond.

Follow this to a junction. Go right and follow the road back to the start.

23 Fortrose to Avoch — C

Old railway lines have a peculiar fascination, cutting a level course through the countryside, and this old track bed between Fortrose and Avoch (pronounced 'Auch') provides a wonderful short walk, high above the Moray Firth. Length: **2 miles/3km** *(one way); Height Climbed:* **160ft/50m**. *Possible link with Walk 22.*

O.S. Sheet 27

From the centre of Fortrose, walk up Station Road. Turn left at the Fire Station and follow Station Crescent as it meanders through the houses. Station Crescent becomes The Orchard, and at the end of The Orchard a path leads onto the old railway.

The railway line once ran from Muir of Ord to Fortrose. It was opened in 1894 and closed in 1960.

Follow the course of the railway through a canopy of trees. There is a fine show of flowers in spring and summer and the going is easy and generally dry underfoot. Wherever there is a gap in the bank to the left of the railway you can look down the steep slope to the Moray Firth and see the curve of houses around the bay in Avoch – a fishing village first developed in the late 16th century.

The railway line ends at the parish church in Avoch, where a signpost points you down the hill to the village centre.

If you don't have anyone to pick you up here, you can return the same way or take a bus back to Fortrose.

Fortrose Cathedral

24 Chanonry Point

An easy walk to one of the best dolphin-spotting sites in Britain. It is also the site of the execution of the Brahan Seer, Scotland's Nostradamus, whose predictions are still treated with respect. Length: **3 miles/5km**; *Height Climbed:* none.

O.S. Sheet 27

From the main street in Fortrose, turn down Academy Street, opposite the Bank of Scotland. Drive past the Cathedral and Fortrose Academy and on down the hill to a small car park and picnic site on the right (no sign).

Walk back on to the road and continue for about 500m, past the caravan site, to a signposted footpath. Follow this path along the shore to the lighthouse at the point. You are beside a golf course, so watch out for golf balls!

At the point there is a car park, a picnic site, and an information board listing the species of seals and dolphins that may be seen. Across the firth is the formidable structure of Fort George: one of the three forts built in the 18th century to control the Great Glen, and the only one that is still a military establishment.

Continue round the point and take the path that leads back towards Fortrose along the shore. If the tide is too high to get round the point, walk a little way down the road from the car park and turn right to join the path (waymarker). When you reach the golf clubhouse, go through the car park and up a minor road onto Ness Road. (Alternatively, continue along the shore to reach Walks 25 & 26).

Cross Ness Road and turn right for

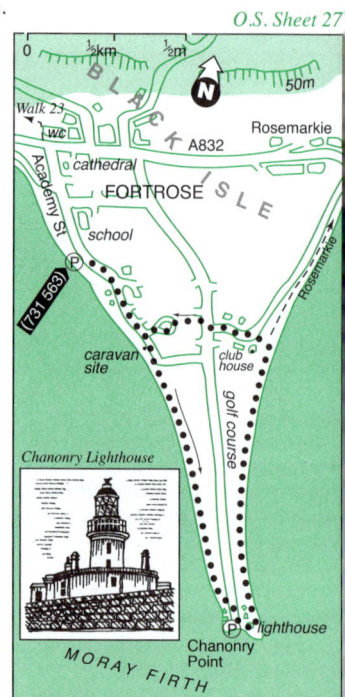

Chanonry Lighthouse

a short distance to reach a sign for a footpath to Wester Links. Turn left on this and follow the path between houses to a public road. Turn left, then left at the next main junction, to rejoin your outward route. Turn right to return to the car park.

25 The Fairy Glen / 26 Scart Craig ──────── C/B

25) *A lineal walk on good paths through a narrow, tree-filled glen with a mill pond and waterfalls. Length:* **2½ miles/4km** *(there and back); Height Climbed:* **150ft/45m**. **26)** *A lineal coastal route leading to cliffs and caves. Length:* **2½ miles/4km** *(there and back); Height Climbed:* **50ft/15m**.

O.S. Sheet 27

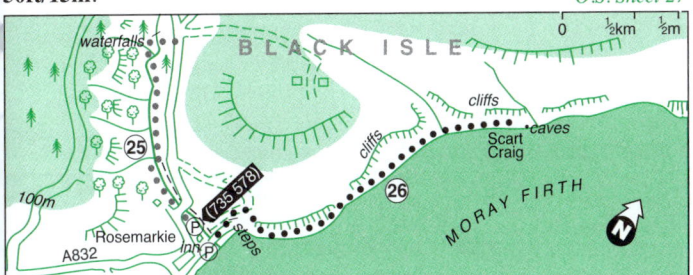

Walk 25) Drive north through Rosemarkie. At the Plough Inn the road turns hard left, and just beyond there is a car park to the right of the road.

Follow the path from the car park upstream, under the road, and continue past a mill pond. This pond once provided water power, water for steeping flax and a supply of ice in the winter.

Continue up the glen. Look for the deeply eroded valleys, or 'dens', on the south side. At the top of the glen there are impressive waterfalls.

Return the same way (or follow the path down the north side of the burn from the bridge).

Walk 26) Drive north through Rosemarkie and turn right at the prominent Plough Inn. Follow the narrow road down to the car park on the shore. (You can also walk out to Chanonry Point (Walk 24) from here.)

From the north end of the car park, go over a footbridge and walk along the shore past a swing park and tennis courts. If the tide is out, you can go onto the beach here. If the tide is in, climb a flight of steps and walk along a path in front of houses. The path then descends gently back down to the shore.

It is easy walking all the way to Scart Craig, along either the path or the beach. The sand has a striking reddish tinge to it, from the Old Red Sandstone rocks. There is plenty of bird life ('scart' means cormorant). Watch also for seals and dolphins.

There are caves at the craig, but if you venture below the cliffs, watch out for the tide. Return the same way.

It is technically possible to walk all way up the coast to Eathie (Walk 29), but this can be hard going and is not possible if the tide is in.

27 South Sutor & The 100 Steps /
28 McFarquhar's Bed _____ B/B

27) *A splendid walk from the attractive 18th-century village of Cromarty, starting along the shore and then climbing steps to the viewpoint at South Sutor. The distance given is out and back, but it is possible to return along the road or link with Walk 28. Length:* **3 miles/5km** *(there and back); Height Climbed:* **400ft/125m**. **28)** *A loop starting on rough paths, visiting a rocky shore with natural arches and caves, and returning along tracks and a quiet public road. Length:* **3½ miles/5.5km**; *Height Climbed:* **330ft/100m**. *(Total length for linked walks:* **5 miles/8km**.) *Be careful of cattle on this route.*

O.S. Sheet 21 or 27

Walk 27) Drive into Cromarty and park in the car park by the shore. Walk east along Shore Street, which soon curves away from the shore (Miller Road). Where the road turns sharp right, turn left down a narrow path and then right along the shore.

Follow a good path along the shore. If you're a fossil hunter, you might prefer to walk along the beach – where Hugh Miller, the famous local geologist, made many of his finds. This is a Site of Special Scientific Interest, and you are asked not to use a geological hammer on any outcrops.

At the end of the beach there is an information board, and the steps start a little way beyond. There is a seat at the top of this first rise, just beyond which the path splits. Keep left. The path meanders through woodland, with occasional small flights of steps. (There are a number of paths through the wood. If the path you are on is overgrown you have missed a turn – double back to find the main path.)

You are now high above the sea and can look across the Moray Firth and down through the trees to the waves breaking on the rocky shore.

On your way, you will pass some wartime fortifications and then a series of steps lead up to the car park at the end of the public road. Return the same way, follow the slightly longer route back to Cromarty by road, or link with Walk 28 (*see* map).

Walk 28) Drive south from Cromarty on Miller Road, leaving the village and climbing to a T-junction. Turn left here, and follow the narrow road to the car park at South Sutor.

Start along the track beyond the car park, which quickly splits. Keep right to reach a gate. A black arrow points ahead-left, and a rough path leads across grazing land and through scattered trees to reach a stile over a fence. Beyond this you are in a more open area, with a fence to your left.

When the cliffs end to your left, the path slants down and across the slope to reach a metal field gate with a stile beside it. Cross this and turn left (arrow) to walk around the edge of a field.

At the end of the field you are at the foot of a line of trees. Just beyond a large fallen tree there is a post with arrows on it. Your return route runs up the line of trees, but to reach McFarquhar's Bed head left on a path running downhill, through a rough grazing area, towards the sea.

The final descent to the shore is steep, and the path zig-zags down the slope, past two old fishing huts, to give a fine view of a stack with an arch in it: McFarquhar's Bed.

Explore the caves along the shore (keeping an eye on the tide), then return to the post in the line of trees. Walk up through the trees. When they end, there is a pedestrian gate beside a field gate directly ahead of you. Go through this and continue, with a fence to your left.

After a few paces you are at the highest point, and a fine view opens up ahead. At the end of the field there is another gate. Go through this and keep straight on, past sheds and houses, to reach the road.

Turn right to return to the start.

29 Eathie _____ B

An easy walk (can be slippy when wet) down to a grassy foreshore and fossil beds by an old salmon fishing station. For the adventurous, it is also the start of a possible coastal walk south to Rosemarkie, although this is dependent on the state of the tide. Length: **3 miles/5km** (there and back); *Height Climbed:* **450ft/140m** (on return).   O.S. Sheet 21 or 27

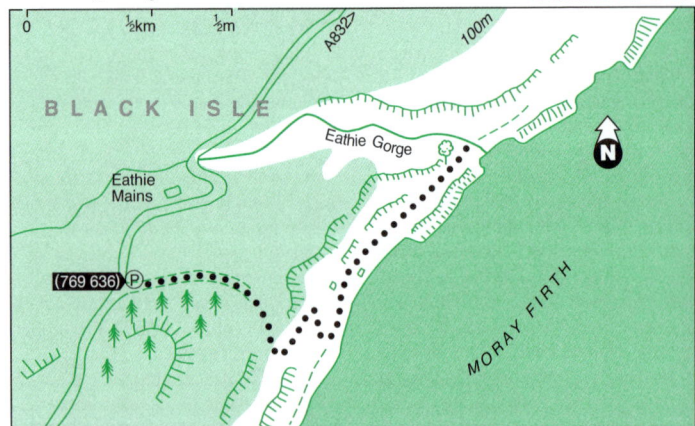

This is one of the fossil sites explored by Hugh Miller (*see* Walk 27) and is also a Site of Special Scientific Interest, so please don't use geological hammers on the outcrops.

About a mile south of Cromarty on the A832, turn off on the minor road signposted for Eathie. Continue along this road for 2½ miles, around the head of Eathie Gorge and past Eathie Mains farm, to a small car park and information board at the start of a conifer plantation on the left.

Follow the broad signposted track along the edge of the trees. After about 500m it starts a steep zig-zag descent through the trees. Where there are gaps in the trees, there are great views across the Moray Firth. As you get closer to the shore, watch out for dolphins and otters.

Head north along the shore, either on the beach or on a faint path through the grass. You will see the slabby fossil beds most clearly at the foot of Eathie Gorge, which is about ½ mile/0.8km away. If you're lucky, you may find something interesting in the shingle.

Return the same way. The route south along the shore to Hillockhead and Rosemarkie is signposted, but this can be hard going and is not possible if the tide is in.